one in two

BY
DONJA R. LOVE

★

★

DRAMATISTS
PLAY SERVICE
INC.

one in two was originally produced in New York City by The New Group (Scott Elliott, Artistic Director; Adam Bernstein, Executive Director) in November 2019. It was directed by Stevie Walker-Webb, the set design was by Arnulfo Maldonado, the costume design was by Qween Jean, the lighting design was by Cha See, the sound design was by Justin Ellington, the video design was by Alex Basco Koch, and the production stage manager was Jakob W. Plummer. The cast was as follows:

PERSON ON THE LEFT .... Jamyl Dobson
PERSON IN THE MIDDLE .... Leland Fowler
PERSON ON THE RIGHT .... Edward Mawere

CHARACTERS

PERSON ON THE LEFT—Black, Male, 20s/30s

PERSON IN THE MIDDLE—Black, Male, 20s/30s

PERSON ON THE RIGHT—Black, Male, 20s/30s

eventually, the above characters become and will remain the below characters

#1—Donté Hart

#2—Mom, Banjii Cunt at the Center, Trade, Person at Bar

#3—Bartender, Nurse, Kinda Ex-Boyfriend, Married Man at the Center

TIME

Now—Until

PLACE

Nowhere, everywhere
(or, a waiting room)

NOTE

This play only needs three actors
(See the following page for more details)

RULES

1. The Audience will choose what actor will play #1. (See page 13.) (Also, since this selection process is randomized and relies solely on The Audience, *all three actors should know every line of text starting on page 13.*)

2. At a certain point (pages 13 and 14), the actors playing Person on the Left, Person in the Middle, and Person on the Right will become #1, #2, and #3. They will remain #1, #2, #3 for the rest of the play.

3. To figure out who will play #2 and #3 after The Audience chooses who will play #1, The Two Unchosen Men will compete in a game. The winner will become #3, and the loser will become #2. (See page 13.)

4. #2 and #3 will play multiple characters, #1 will not.

5. None of the actors should "pretend" to be any of the characters. No stereotypes or caricatures. That shit is corny, and this play deserves better. All you have to do is just…be.

> 5a. Don't think of this play and the characters herein as heavy, serious, or sad because of the subject matter. That will get you but so far. Yes, those moments do exist, but so does the comedy. Basically, you don't have to cry or add those dramatic ass pauses. Dear God, please don't add them! As a rule of thumb: *These people (in this play and in real life) laugh just as much as they cry.*

6. This one isn't a rule. It's more of an earnest request. Please cast someone living with HIV in this play. Please. I know this may be incredibly tricky and sensitive due to shame and stigmatization, but how affirming would it be to have someone living with HIV in one of the roles? Or two? Or all three?

Before starting a play, I've always needed a quote, whether written or visual, to guide me into the world that's being created. For this play, however, nothing came to me. For months I mulled over quotes, but nothing stuck. Then, I started thinking about when I'd apply for playwriting fellowships, residencies, awards, etc. There was one paragraph I'd put in every artistic statement.

> *"There is still trauma that's hard to write; there are still remnants of fear that tremble the voice found in my writing. I've gotten to a point where there are no words, characters, dialogue, or subtext to hide behind anymore. Fear can no longer overshadow the truth. And the truth is, I've been too afraid to share I'm HIV positive. Ironically, for so long, I'd create stories surrounding HIV, but I would never admit that those stories are authentic to me."*

After rereading that paragraph, I realized I found my way into this play.

“While we wait” (Pre-show)

Waiting room music plays. As people enter, they take a number from the ticket dispenser, which is located directly by the room’s entrance(s). There are only three numbers that the machine continuously dispenses: one, two, three. After taking a number, everyone sits and waits.

one in two

We see…
Three Black men, who have been quietly waiting.
They're trapped in an open, all-white (waiting) room. It's pristine, sterile, and clinical. The men are only wearing pants.
We hear…
The kind of music you hear in a waiting room.
This waiting goes on for a while. As it does, right above the men, a single number floats: Zero. Eventually, the floating number begins to increase one number at a time.
The Numbers will continue to do such for the rest of the play.
The Numbers continue to rise.
Tick.

Tick.

Tick.

PERSON ON THE LEFT.
(Simultaneously.)
Wait!

PERSON IN THE MIDDLE.
(Simultaneously.)
Fuck!

PERSON ON THE RIGHT.
(Simultaneously.)
Again?!

The ticking gets louder.

PERSON ON THE LEFT.
(Simultaneously.)
Can you give me a second?!

PERSON IN THE MIDDLE.
(Simultaneously.)
I'm not a number!

PERSON ON THE RIGHT.
(Simultaneously.)
I'm not ready!

The ticking gets louder.

ALL THREE MEN. Wait! Please!

The ticking gets louder.

FINE!

A (white) ticket dispenser appears. The men stare at it for a while, frightened. Then:

PERSON ON THE RIGHT. Who's going to pull first?

Person on the Left and Person in the Middle don't move.

Fine. I will.

Person on the Right goes to the ticket dispenser and pulls a number. After a moment, Person on the Left and Person in the Middle also pull a number.

PERSON IN THE MIDDLE. Maaaaan, fuck.

PERSON ON THE RIGHT. What? What number did you get?

Person in the Middle shows Person on the Left and Person on the Right his number.

PERSON ON THE LEFT and PERSON ON THE RIGHT. Oh.

PERSON IN THE MIDDLE. I know.

PERSON ON THE LEFT. I mean… I don't, I don't think it's anything wrong with that one.

PERSON IN THE MIDDLE. Yeah, it's not, but I pulled this one last time.

PERSON ON THE RIGHT. And I pulled this one last time.

PERSON IN THE MIDDLE. So?!

PERSON ON THE RIGHT. *So* you don't see me bitchin'.

PERSON IN THE MIDDLE. I'm not bitchin', nigga. I'm just… I'm tired of doing it this way. Picking from that ticket dispenser to figure out who's gonna…you know, be who and do what. All while stuck in this waiting room, waiting. Let's switch it up. Figure out a different system or something.

PERSON ON THE LEFT. But, but we always do it this way.

PERSON IN THE MIDDLE. Well, not this time.

PERSON ON THE RIGHT. So then, what are you proposing?

Person in the Middle looks out at The Audience and smiles. Person on the Right points to The Audience.

Them?

PERSON IN THE MIDDLE. Yup! We're here because of them. So why not?

PERSON ON THE RIGHT. No.

PERSON IN THE MIDDLE. What you mean "no"?

PERSON ON THE RIGHT. We can't just switch up how we do things.

PERSON IN THE MIDDLE. Says who? *(Looks around.)* It's nobody here, but us.

PERSON ON THE LEFT. *(Points to The Audience.)* And, and them.

PERSON ON THE RIGHT. And you're trying to get them to be a part of it.

PERSON IN THE MIDDLE. Just this one time, for this one thing, I want to try. That's it. I mean, they're here, busy watching what's happening anyway. So why not? Please?

Person on the Right thinks.

PERSON ON THE RIGHT. …Fine. But just this one time.

PERSON IN THE MIDDLE. Cool. Let's do this!

PERSON ON THE LEFT. How, how do we do *this*?

PERSON IN THE MIDDLE. So, we're gonna stand in a straight line, right? Then one of us will take a step forward, *(Points to The Audience.)* they'll clap for that person, then that person who stepped forward will take a step back into the line. The next person will take a step forward; they'll clap for that person, then that person will take a step back into the line. Theeeen—

PERSON ON THE RIGHT. Let me guess…they'll take a step forward, *(Points to The Audience.)* they'll clap for that person, then that person will take a step back into the line?

PERSON IN THE MIDDLE. Exactly! And whoever gets the loudest claps will be Number One.

Beat.

So y'all got it?

PERSON ON THE RIGHT and PERSON ON THE LEFT. Yeah.

PERSON IN THE MIDDLE. Not y'all. I know y'all got it. I'm talking about them. *(Points to The Audience.)* Y'all got it?

Waits for a response. In the event of no response, Person in the Middle says something like: "Alright, imma ask y'all again, do y'all got it?" or "Imma need some energy from y'all!" or "Y'all got it. It's not that damn hard!" etc.

They're on board.

PERSON ON THE RIGHT. So, like, what are they clapping for?

PERSON IN THE MIDDLE. What you mean?

PERSON ON THE RIGHT. Like…are they clapping for who's the…

PERSON ON THE LEFT. Most popular?!

PERSON ON THE RIGHT. Or the strongest?!

PERSON ON THE LEFT. Or smartest?!

PERSON ON THE RIGHT. Or sexiest?!

PERSON IN THE MIDDLE. Does it matter?

Beat.

PERSON ON THE RIGHT. No, I guess not. Fine. Come on.

PERSON IN THE MIDDLE. Yeah. Let's do this!

They stand side by side.

(To The Audience.) Remember, no qualifiers. Just clap for whoever you want and clap as loud as you want.

Person in the Middle takes a step out. The Audience claps. Person steps back in line.

Person on the Right steps out. The Audience claps. Person steps back in line.

Person on the Left steps out. The Audience claps. Person steps back in line.

A moment.

The three men stand there, taking in the new selection "system."

ALL THREE MEN. Yooooooo.

Another moment.

Woooooow.

Again, the person who received the loudest applause becomes #1. A red light shines on who The Audience selected to be #1.

#1. *(In disbelief.)* So…so, I'm Number One?

THE TWO UNCHOSEN MEN. Yeah.

#1. Nope. Nope. I'm not doing it.

THE TWO UNCHOSEN MEN. But you have to.

#1. No, I don't. Nope. Not doing it. Get The Audience to pick again.

The Two Unchosen Men stare at The Numbers then at #1 like: "Nigga. Now you know that ain't happenin'. Stop actin' like a lil' bitch."

Ugh! Fine. I'm Number One. Okay? Happy? Stop staring at me and figure out who's gonna be Number Two and who will be Number Three between you two.

THE TWO UNCHOSEN MEN. Okay.

The Two Unchosen Men grab hands.

Rock,
paper,
scissors,
shoot!

They begin to play. Whoever wins will become #3, and whoever loses will become #2.

#3. Boo-ya! Since I won, I'll be Numbeeeeeeeer Two. No! No, no. Scratch that. Imma be Number Three? *(Maybe thinks about all Number Three's roles.)* You know what, on third thought, I think imma actual-ly, realistical-ly, in all hones-ty be…

#1. If you don't hurry up and pick!

#3. Damn. Calm down. I was just gonna say… Imma stay Number Three.

#1. And you can't change it.

#3. I won't. I like this role.

#1. Okay. So, then, *(Points to the loser of "Rock, Paper, Scissors!")* you're Number Two.

#2. Okay.

#1 goes over to a box and takes out three shirts.
We notice that each shirt has a different number on it: 1, 2, 3.
#1 starts giving out the shirts. The men put the clothing on.
Just so we're super clear: The person who got the loudest applause wears the shirt with the 1 on it, the person who won "Rock, Paper, Scissors!" gets the shirt with the 3 on it, and the loser of the game gets the shirt with the 2 on it.

#3. Let's get this show on the road!

#2. Wait. Shouldn't we, shouldn't we tell them, like, who we are first? *(Points to The Audience.)* So they don't just see us as a number.

#1. It doesn't matter. Let's start as kids this time.

#2 and #3. Okay.

They start running all over the space, which may transform in appearance and color.
As they run, we watch them transform into little kids around five and six years old. Then, after carefree running and laughing, they all sit down in a triangle.
#3 gets up.

#3. *(As a kid.)* I'll start!

He circles #1 and #2. He begins touching their heads.

Duck, duck, duck, duck, duck, goo-duck!
Duck, duck, duck, duck, duuuuuuuuuuuuuuuck, duck.

He chooses #2.

GOOSE!

They run around in a circle, and #3 quickly grabs #2's seat. #2 begins to circle #1 and #3. He begins touching their heads.

#2. *(As a kid.)* Duck, duck.

He chooses #3.

GOOSE!

They run around in a circle, and #2 quickly grabs #3's seat. #3 begins to circle #1 and #2. He begins touching their heads.

#3. *(As a kid.)* Duuuuuuuuuck, duuuuuuuuuck, duuuuuuck, duuu uuuuuuuuuuuuuuuuuuuuuuuuuuuuck.

He chooses #2.

GOOSE!

#1. *(Grown-up version.)* Not fair, not fair, not fair! Yo, I never get picked for this shit. I don't wanna do this anymore. I'm done! Hmph!

#3. *(Grown-up version.)* Really?

#1. *(Grown-up version.)* Really. *(Looking at The Numbers.)* I'm not just a number. I'm flesh. I'm blood. I feel.

#2. *(Grown-up version.)* True.

#3. *(Grown-up version.)* But—

#2. *(Grown-up version.)* I'm done, too.

#3. *(Grown-up version.)* But—

#1. *(Grown-up version.)* "But" nothing. We're done. If you're gonna keep us in here, we're gonna control what we do and how this shit go from now on. *(To The Numbers.)* Not you!

#2. *(To The Numbers.)* Yeah. We're…we're taking a stand!

The ticking gets louder.

(To The Numbers.) So what.

The ticking gets louder.

#1. *(To The Numbers.)* We don't care.

The ticking gets louder.

(To The Numbers.) You can tick all you want. We're done.

The ticking gets so loud it becomes deafening.

ALL THREE. AHHHHHH!

The men, all in extreme pain, cover their ears in hopes to drown out the sound.
It doesn't work.

#1. *(To The Numbers.)* OKAY! OKAY! OKAY!

The loud ticking continues, as The Numbers increase.

(As a kid, fearful, forcing a big ass smile.) OKAY!

#3. Maybe we shouldn't—

#1. Let's go back to kids and play another game!

#2. *(As a kid.)* What you wanna play?

#1. *(As a kid.)* Um, uh… *(Thinks.)* Let's play… *(Whispers.)* "I'll show you mine if you show me yours."

A moment.

#3. *(As a kid.)* That's gay.

#1. *(As a kid.)* Nah-uhn.

#3. *(As a kid.)* Yeah, it is.

#1. *(As a kid.)* Only if we kiss it.
I think?

#2. *(As a kid.)* Really?

#1. *(As a kid.)* Really.

#3. *(As a kid.)* Nah-uhn!

#1. *(As a kid.)* Uhn-huhn! My uncle told me that.

#2. *(As a kid.)* Really?

#1. *(As a kid.)* Really.

#2. *(As a kid.)* Oh, okay!

#3. *(As a kid.)* Well… I guess.

They stand. No one moves. After awkward silence:

You was, is supposed to go first since you wanted to play this.

#1. *(As a kid.)* Oh, yeah, right!

Nervously, he pulls his pants down, showing his privates to the other boys. Their mouths drop.

Then, they laugh big ole laughs.

What? What's so funny?

#2. *(As a kid.)* I don't know. Outside of mine, I never saw another one before.

#1. *(As a kid.)* Really?

#2. *(As a kid.)* Really.

#1. *(As a kid.)* Well, this mine. I named it!

#2. *(As a kid.)* Really?

#1. *(As a kid.)* Really.

#3. *(As a kid.)* What you name it?

#1. *(As a kid.)* Mighty Morphing Power Rangers!

#3. *(As a kid.)* You can't name it that!

#1. *(As a kid.)* Yes, I can.

#3. *(As a kid.)* No, you can't!

#1. *(As a kid.)* Yes, I can!

#3. *(As a kid.)* No!

#1. *(As a kid.)* Yes!

#3. *(As a kid.)* No!

#1. *(As a kid.)* Yes!

#3. *(As a kid.)* Nooooooooo!

#1. *(As a kid.)* Yesssssssss!

#3 balls up his fist to hit #1. #1 notices so he balls up his fist, too. #2 notices so he quickly pulls his pants down, showing his privates to the other boys.

#2. *(As a kid.)* Look! Look! This one is mine!

The other two look.

#1 and #3. *(As kids.)* Woooooooow!

#2. *(As a kid.)* I know! And I named it Rugrats!

#1. *(As a kid.)* Rugrats?

#2. *(As a kid.)* Yeah, I like that show. And I like my dick.

#1. *(As a kid.)* Ooooooooooool. You cursed.

#2. *(As a kid.)* Dick is not a curse word 'cause it's a part of your body.

My dad says it all the time. Especially at night when I hear him tell my mom, "Suck my dick."

#3. *(As a kid.)* Suck my dick!

They laugh.

#2. *(As a kid.)* Suck *my* dick.

#3. *(As a kid.)* Suck my *dick*!

#2 and #3 run over to #1.

#2 and #3. *(As kids.)* Say it,
say it,
say it!

#1. *(As a kid.)* Dick.

Embarrassed, #1 quickly covers his mouth. #2 and #3 laugh with excitement.

Suck. My. Diiiiiiiick!

#2 and #3. *(As kids.)* Yaaaaay!

They begin marching like soldiers.

Dick, dick, dick, dick, dick.

#1 joins them in marching and singing.

#1, #2, and #3. *(As kids.)* Dick, dick, dick, dick, dick.

#1. *(As a kid.)* Now, show us your dick!

#1 and #2. *(As kids.)* Show us your dick!
Show us your dick!
Show us your dick!
Show us your dick!
Show us your dick!

#3. *(As a kid.)* Okay, okay, okay, already.

#3 pulls his pants down, like the other two, and shows his privates to the other boys.

#2. *(As a kid.)* Aw. It looks so nice.

#3. *(As a kid.)* Thank you.

#1. *(As a kid.)* I can tell you take good care of it.

#3. *(As a kid.)* I do!

#2. *(As a kid.)* What's its name?

#3. *(As a kid.)* Uh, its name?

#1. *(As a kid.)* Yeah. What do you call it?

#3. *(As a kid.)* Um…um… I call it…um…Donté.

#1. *(As a kid.)* Donté? You can't call it that!

#3. *(As a kid.)* Why can't I? I like that name. So yeah! This is Donté, and you or you won't and can't change that. Not now and not ever! Not in a million or kah-gillion years! Hmph!

A moment, they stare at him.

#1 and #2. *(As kids.)* Okay.

#1. *(As a kid.)* Can we finish playing?

#2. *(As a kid.)* Yeah!

They pull up their pants, a moment.

#1. *(As a kid.)* What should we play?

#3. *(As a kid.)* Ol, ol! I know. Let's play, "So an HIV-positive man walks into a bar!"

#1. *(As a kid.)* I never heard of that one.

#3. *(As a kid.)* Really?

#1. *(As a kid.)* Really.

#3. *(As a kid.)* Okay. So, since you're Number One, you'll be the HIV-positive man that walks into the bar. Okay?

#1. *(As a kid.)* Uhhh, okay.

#3. *(As a kid.)* All you gotta do is walk into the bar, sit down, and drink. But you gotta drink a lot! Okay?

#1. *(As a kid.)* Okay. Am I with anyone, like my mommy or daddy or somebody?

#3. *(As a kid.)* No. Just you.

#1. *(As a kid.)* Okay. Well, why am I drinking?

#3. *(As a kid.)* Because you're sad.

#1. *(As a kid.)* Oh, okay. And what happens when I'm done drinking?

#3. *(As a kid.)* You kill yourself.

Beat.

#1. *(As a kid.)* Okay.

#3. *(As a kid.)* Now let's play! So, an HIV-positive man walks into a bar…

They all begin to create a bar. The counter, the stools, tables, everything. Or maybe it all just appears, or maybe we just use our imagination.

#3 becomes the bartender, #1 becomes the man who walks into the bar. As they're doing this, right before our very eyes, we watch them grow into men.

All the while, The Numbers still increase.

Beat.

#1 sits at the bar, drinking.

#1. *(To Bartender, drunk.)* Hey, hey, hey. HEY!

#3. *(As Bartender.)* Yes, *Donté.*

#1. Wait, wait, wait! We never gave anyone a name before. So, like, how are you just gonna randomly give me one now?

#3. Because, ummm, we're telling a story. Duh. *(Points to The Audience.)* And they need an easily identifiable protagonist to follow, to help them make sense of an already amorphous, challenging, and borderline nonexistent ass plot. Plus, I like the name Donté. So… deal.

#1. *(As Donté.)* Fine.

A moment, maybe to get back into the groove of things.

When I was little, I useta show my dick to my friends all the time. You ever do that, BARTENDER?!

#3 cheerily gives #1 a thumbs up like, "Good job for naming me and seeing the importance in giving me a name, even if your petty ass really didn't give me a name."

#3. *(As Bartender.)* Yeah.

#1. *(As Donté, still drunk.)* You wanna, you wanna see my dick?

#3. *(As Bartender.)* As much as I would love to, I gotta get other people feeling good, too. Not just you.

#2 walks in and sits. Bartender goes over to him.

Hey, how can I hel—

#2. Wait, wait, wait.

Waiting room music may play.

#3. What?

#2. I really don't wanna… I mean, like, do we have to do this? Do we really have to…do we really have to tell *this* story again?

#3 looks at The Numbers increase.

#3. Yeah. Now come on.

#2. Wait. Well. Now that all three of us are in it, before we keep going, I think maybe this time we should come up with a safe word.

#3. A safe word?

#2. Yeah. I mean, we, we already switched things up by having The Audience be a part of this. So, so we can switch things up again by, by adding a safe word?

#3. We don't need one.

#2. For when things get too real, I think we do.

#1. That kinda makes sense.

#2. I… I just want to make sure you're okay. That's all.

#2 shoots #1 a nervous smile.

#3. Okay. Whatever. The safe word is…"stop."

#2. It can't be "stop."

#3. Why?

#2. That's so on the nose. And we could be saying "stop" for like anything.

#3. True dat.

#1. I got it! Our safe word can be "HIV."

#2. HIV? Really? You want that to be the safe word?

#1. Yeah.

#3. HIV cannot be the safe word.

#1. …

#3. …

#1. What?

#3. You know how that sounds, right?

#1. How?

#3. Like high-key stigma. HIV in the same sentence as "not safe." You tried it.

#1. I ain't even mean it like that.

#3. Plus, the safe word can't be what this whole thing is about. It's like…they tell women if they ever get raped, never scream "rape" because motherfuckers won't come, but if you scream "fire," they'll run to save ya ass.

#1. Oh shit.

#3. I know.

#2. So what can we have the word be?

#3. Let me think.

#3 thinks. Hard. He maybe even motions his pointer finger in the air as if he's solving a tough math problem by carrying the two.

#1. Sooooo.

#3. I'm thinking. Damn, nigga!

Beat.

I got it!

#2. What?

#3. The safe word is…"niggaaaaaaa."

#1. Nigga?

#3. No.

#2. But you just said "nigga."

#3. No I didn't.

#1. Yes, you did.

#3. No, I said…"niggaaaaaaa." Seven "A"s.

#1 and #2. *(Annoyed.)* Nigga!

#3. For real. That's our safe word!

#1. …

#3. …

#1. Fine. Niggaaaaaa.

#3. You missed an "A."

#3 looks at #1, waiting.

#1. ...ah.

#3. My nigga!

#2. But we say that word so much. What if, what if we get confused?

#3. Please. We know the beautiful nuances of "nigga." So we won't, my nigga.

#2. Okay. We have a safe word. Let's, let's jump back in it.

They reposition themselves at the bar.

#1. Wait.

#3. Oh my God! Now what?! We can't keep stopping. Y'all remember what happened to us earlier when we tried to stop this?!

#1. It's just that we gotta start from the beginning now.

#3. Why?

#1. All the stopping and starting took me out of it. Now I gotta rework myself up to the suicide.

#2. You sure?

#1. Yeah.

#2. Okay.

#2 exits the playing space as #3 undresses and walks over to #1. #3 begins kissing #1's neck.

#1. What are you doing?

#3. Kissing you?

#1. Why?

#3. So we can fuck.

#1. Why?

#3. Aren't we doing the part when you...contract it?

#1. No. We don't have to fu...we don't have to start there. Let's just start when I find out.

#3. You sure? 'Cause I'm ready to be that hookup who put it down.

#1. I'm sure.

#3. Suit yourself.

#2 brings out a desk, chairs, and a wall adorned with HIV

posters and pamphlets. Or maybe it all just appears, or maybe we just use our imagination. #1 sits silently as #3 grabs nurse scrubs, puts them on, and sits at the desk. On a good day, this nurse is a ray of sunshine. On a bad day, the nurse hates this job and everyone there. We can't tell what kinda day it is.

(As Nurse.) With all the advancements we've made, this is no longer a death sentence.

Donté says nothing. The nurse hands him a pamphlet.

There are some meds where you only have to take one pill a day.

Donté says nothing.

We have a program here for those who are positive that you can attend. It's always a good turnout. And it's really helpful, and there are snacks.

Donté says nothing.

I know this is a lot to handle, but you can get through this, Mr. Hart. Your status will not be the most interesting thing about you.

Donté says nothing.

You have access now, resources, information. Not everyone does. Not everyone in your position can get this help. Some people are out there living with this virus and don't even know it, and if they do, they don't even have the means to do anything about it. So you are good. Okay? I'll set you an appointment with one of the doctors we have here at the center.

The nurse begins looking through files.

I can set you up with Doctor Number One next Thursday at three P.M. Darnit, you know what, he's actually starting his Christmas vacation a week early so he'll be out. Hm. Maybe Doctor Number Two? No, she'll be out, too. And so will Doctor Number Three. Hm, we're in a pickle. The holidays. Ahhhh! Scheduling nightmare. I got it. I'll have Doctor Number Four meet with you. Next Thursday work?

Donté says nothing.

Look, everything will be okay. Okay? I mean, yes, your life will be a bit different, but overall it'll be the same. Nothing will *really* change. When I found out I had diabetes, I thought everything would be different, but it wasn't. I still eat cornbread, collard greens, macaroni and cheese, fried chicken, smothered chicken, pork chops, hog maws, ham hocks, yams, sweet potato pie, banana pudding, rice pudding, peach cobbler, blackberry cobbler, snickerdoodle cobbler, snickerdoodle cookies, pineapple upside-down cake, and drink sweet tea to wash it all down. Okay?!

#1. *(As Donté.)* But this isn't diabetes.

A moment.

I need to tell my mom and my boyfriend. Well, he's not my boyfriend anymore. I broke up with him a few months ago because I thought it's somebody better out there for me, but me and him, we still…he won't want to do that anymore.

Donté is emotional. A moment, then #3 starts taking off the scrubs.

#3. I don't want to be the mom.

#2 quietly comes out.

#2. If you don't have to then neither, neither do I.

#1. Well, somebody's gotta do it.

#3. Let's have The Audience decide.

#1. No. That was that one time we used them. Y'all can have our tried and true method figure out who's gonna play her.

#3. Fine.

#2 and #3. One
two
three
four
I declare a thumb war!

#2 loses.

#3. Yeeeeeea, boi. I'm on a roll!

#2. Ugh, whatever.

#3 begins to dance.

#3. Ayeeeeeee, ayeeeeeee, ayeeeeeee, ayeeeeeee!

#2. Can you calm down? Like, is everything a joke to you?

#3. Ummm? Yeah.

He continues dancing.

#1. Chill out, Number Three. Okay? And you'll be fine, Number Two. If it helps, Number Three already played a woman.

#3. Really?

#1. Yeah.

#3. Who?

#1. The nurse.

#3. Oh.

#1. *(To #2.)* You'll be fine as the mom, okay? All you gotta do for real for real is just…*be.*

#3. Who you wanna tell first? Mom or Kinda Ex-Boyfriend?

#1. *(Nervous.)* I don't know.

#2. It might be best to tell Kinda Ex-Boyfriend first, maybe?

#1. Yeah. Okay. I'll tell him first.

He breathes.
Then…
#3 comes up behind him, gently wraps his arms around him, and lays them both down. He just holds #1, as they quietly lay.

#3. *(As Kinda Ex-Boyfriend.)* I still love you.

#1. *(As Donté.)* Really?

#3. *(As Kinda Ex-Boyfriend.)* Of course. How could I not?

#1. *(As Donté.)* I just thought…

#3. *(As Kinda Ex-Boyfriend.)* Well, don't think that.

Beat.

#1. *(As Donté.)* You should go and get tested.

#3. *(As Kinda Ex-Boyfriend.)* I did.

#1. *(As Donté.)* Really?

#3. *(As Kinda Ex-Boyfriend.)* Yeah.

#1. *(As Donté.)* When?

#3. *(As Kinda Ex-Boyfriend.)* Last week.

#1. *(As Donté.)* And?

#3. *(As Kinda Ex-Boyfriend.)* I don't.

#1. *(As Donté.)* Oh. Well… God, or whoever's up there, must really love you.

#3. *(As Kinda Ex-Boyfriend.)* And not you?

Donté honestly doesn't have an answer.

I've been having this dream lately. It's always the same, me leading praise and worship when the church starts to shake. I think it's the holy spirit or something until everyone disappears like it's the rapture. Eventually, I realize I'm left behind. I start thinking it's because of what we do. But as soon as I think that God shows up. And God doesn't look how we think God looks. God looks like… I don't know, the last time you smiled, maybe? And the more I'm looking at God, the more I see you, the more I see that you are loved that you are love. *My* love.

Donté becomes emotional.

Everything will be okay. You'll get through this. We'll get through this. I'm not going anywhere.

#1. *(As Donté.)* You mean that.

#3. *(As Kinda Ex-Boyfriend.)* On God.

They kiss.
Kinda Ex-Boyfriend begins to sing "Hold to God's Unchanging Hand," or something like that.
#2, now as Mom, enters and sings the same song Kinda Ex-Boyfriend is singing. Mom sits as Kinda Ex-Boyfriend exits. Donté just writes in a notebook as all this happens around him. Eventually, he notices Mom, who just sings.

#1. *(As Donté.)* Mom?

Mom just sings.

Mom?

Mom just sings.

Mom!

Mom stops singing, silence.

Say something. Please.

#2. *(As Mom.)* Something like what? What you say when your son tells you he has…

She can't say it, but her body feels it. You know that saying, "You look like you were hit by a Mack truck?"
That's exactly what Mom feels, how she looks. She stares off.
She can't even look at her son.
More silence, as The Numbers increase.

I always told you to be careful.

#1. *(As Donté.)* I know.

#2. *(As Mom.)* I always told you don't get lost out there in the world, baby.

#1. *(As Donté.)* I know.

#2. *(As Mom.)* But here you are…lost.
How that happen?

#1. *(As Donté.)* I don't know.

#2. *(As Mom.)* My baby. My firstborn.

She's overcome with emotion. Donté, filled with equal parts hope and strength, consoles his mom and wipes away her tears.

#1. *(As Donté.)* It'll be okay, Mom. Don't worry. Everything's gonna be okay. I promise.

#2. *(As Mom.)* I just don't want you to hurt. That's all this is.

#1. *(As Donté.)* I'll make it through. There's a group for other people who's also…imma start going there.

#2. *(As Mom.)* That's good. You'll have people to talk to. People who been in ya shoes.

#1. *(As Donté.)* I will.

#2. *(As Mom.)* Outside of that group, don't talk to anybody else about this. You keep this to yourself. You hear me, Donté? Folks ain't too kind about this. They ain't too kind about anything actually.

#1. *(As Donté.)* I will.

#2. *(As Mom.)* Good. You eat? You need to eat. You probably so hungry. You should eat something. Let me cook my baby something to eat.

#1. *(As Donté.)* Okay.

She continues to cry and sing/hum as she exits.
Donté, now alone, begins to write in his notebook as a way

of stopping himself from crying until...
#2 comes back out, voguing. #3 also comes out carrying chairs. The space becomes a center.

#2. *(As Banjii Cunt at the Center.)* I love coming to this center or whateva. It's real cute. Liiiiike, she help down! Okay? Having a community, or whateva, and being around other poz folx, this shit is lifesaviiiiiing because a bitch didn't think she could make it. No shade.

#3. *(As Married Man at the Center.)* Yeah. My husband, though he's super supportive, it can be difficult at times. With us being in a sero-discordant marriage.

#2. *(As Banjii Cunt at the Center.)* What the fuck is that?

#3. *(As Married Man at the Center.)* A neutral relationship. He's negative, and I'm positive.

#2. *(As Banjii Cunt at the Center.)* Gurl, why you ain't just say that then?

#3. *(As Married Man at the Center.)* Because I said sero-discordant instead.

#2. *(As Banjii Cunt at the Center.)* Oop. Don't get cute 'cause we got new people here, Mister Married Man at the Center.

#3. *(As Married Man at the Center.)* I'm not. I'm just letting you know.

Beat.

And another thing that makes it hard is his mom. I've never met her, but she is *always* present.

#2. *(As Banjii Cunt at the Center.)* How? And why ain't you neva meet her?

#3. *(As Married Man at the Center.)* She, um, she doesn't like the fact that her son is with me because I'm poz.

#2. *(As Banjii Cunt at the Center.)* Damn.

#3. *(As Married Man at the Center.)* I know. It's...it's so...infuriating. I have a good job. I'm good to her son. I'm a good person. It's like none of that matters. Not even him being on PrEP, me being undetectable, and us always using protection. There's absolutely no way I can transmit it to him. I just... I wish she... I wish she would let go of her antiquated ignorance to understand that.

#2. *(As Banjii Cunt at the Center.)* Sis, I keep telling you, you need to be like me and not care what people think about ya status. And, like, *you* really shouldn't care. You got you a man. So forget about his mama. You ain't fuckin' that bitch.

Married Man at the Center just stares at Banjii Cunt at the Center.

What?!

#3. *(As Married Man at the Center.)* Why do you always have to act like this, Banjii Cunt at the Center? We have new people here, so be less…banjii.

#2. *(As Banjii Cunt at the Center.)* Pay it. And heeeeey new person. What's goodie?! I'm Banjii Cunt at the Center. I love long walks in the park, after dark. Owww! Sike nah, but really, I love spendin' time with the ones I love. I love red Kool-Aid. The smell of a laundromat, as you can imagine, it just smell so refreshing or whateva. Uh, what else? Oh yeah, I love when my haters see me win cuz they be gaggin'. Aaaaaaaaand I'm currently a 007.

#3. *(As Married Man at the Center, to Donté.)* He's deep in the ballroom culture.

#2. *(As Banjii Cunt at the Center.)* Yes the fuck I is. One of the up-and-comin' legendary children, and I'm currently scopin' out what house to join, so if you have any suggestions holla at cha gurl.

He goes back to voguing.

#3. *(As Married Man at the Center.)* And I'm Married Man at the Center.

#1. *(As Donté.)* Hi.

#3. *(As Married Man at the Center.)* Hi. What's your name?

#1. *(As Donté.)* Donté.

#3. *(As Married Man at the Center.)* Hi Donté. When did you find out?

#1. *(As Donté.)* Two weeks ago.

#3. *(As Married Man at the Center.)* And how has everything been? How have *you* been?

#1. *(As Donté.)* Um. Blurry. I think. I mean, if I can even describe myself that way. Like I need to clean my eyes or something because nothing looks right or feels right anymore. Everything's so smudged into everything. And I just feel like a blur. The medicine my doctor gave me doesn't help. It makes me feel like shit. So I stopped taking it. And I know you're probably thinking, "You have to take your meds or you'll die." But my meds actually made this ankle swell two times larger than this ankle. No one tells you that shit like that might happen. They just tell you, "Take your meds!" So I did. And it became incredibly hard to walk, which caused major problems because another side effect of my meds was constantly having to shit. But it hurts like hell just walking a few feet to the bathroom. While all this was happening, the guy who I was kinda with when I found out, Kinda Ex-Boyfriend is his name, he took it really well. And even though he doesn't have it, he still made sure that nothing would change between us. He told me he still loves me. When I told him, he held me all night and sang to me. And the next morning before he left for work, he gave me the most alive kiss that I've ever tasted. When I called him later that day because I really needed to hear his voice, he didn't answer. When I texted him, he never responded. I haven't seen him since I told him. I actually kinda wonder if I even did see him then, if I just made it all up. If I made up the three years with him because he just disappeared like it never existed. Maybe it would've been best if I didn't tell him. If he didn't know, if I didn't know. Ya know? And speaking of what doesn't exist, my sex drive doesn't. Like, you would think it owes me money because it's nowhere to be found.

He laughs?

It's really not funny. It's actually sad, pathetic even. I could fuck anytime, anywhere, as much as I breathed in a day, but now...nope. All I do is cry. The one thing that helps, though, is writing. I'm a playwright, or at least I wanted to be. I'm writing this dreamlike play that's set in the middle of nowhere and nothing. Or maybe a waiting room? Because that wait has so much weight to it. Ya know? It just feels like you're waiting forever, and you're trapped in your own head, so everything and everyone starts to blur. But I don't know. I probably won't do anything with it, though. I'll be too scared to share it with anyone, to have people possibly rehearse it, audiences watch it, and critics critique it. Something so personal. I don't know. And just saying it aloud, it sounds pretty stupid, so I may stop writing it.

Banjii Cunt at the Center and Married Man at the Center just stare at Donté.
Until:

#2. *(As Banjii Cunt at the Center.)* Yup. Welcome to the club, boo.

Beat.
Donté pulls out his notebook and begins to write. He just writes and writes and writes. But he begins to have trouble writing and starts violently ripping out page after page after page.
Seeing him struggle, #2 begins to take Donté's clothes off and puts him in bed.
Donté sleeps as #2 waits.
And waits.
And waits.
Then, after it seems #2 has been waiting forever…
#2 gets Donté out of bed and dresses him in new clothes. The whole time this is happening, Donté drinks.
After dressing him, #2 begins to leave.

#1. *(As Donté, drunk.)* What time is it?

#2. *(Looks at the time.)* Five years later.

#1. *(As Donté.)* Really?

The Numbers significantly increase. Beat.

#2. Yeah.

Donté looks at the bottle in his hand.

#1. *(As Donté.)* And all I've done, for five years, was drink?

#2. Yeah.

#2 exits the playing space.
Donté drinks. He grabs a bottle of prescription pills—his meds—and just stares at them. He opens the bottle and takes a pill. As soon as he puts it in his mouth, he begins to gag. The gagging is so painful and pill so hard to swallow that he spits it out. He continues to drink as he grabs his phone and makes a call.

#1. *(As Donté, drunk.)* Hello.

Space indicates talking on the other end of the phone.

Hey, Booty Call Number One.

Right, right. Booty Call Number Two. I know you're Booty Call Number Two. I was joking.

Beat—probably silence on the other end.

What you doing later?

Oh. What time you get off?

Wanna come over after?

Yeah, yeah, yeah, that totally makes sense. I'll probably be tired, too, since you get off so late.

No, no. It's cool. I'll talk to you later. Bye.

He quickly hangs up the phone; then, he makes another call.
It rings and rings and rings.
He drinks.

Pick up, pick up. Please.

They don't pick up.

Fuck.

He tries to put on sexy voice.

Hey, Booty Call Number Three. It's me… Donté. I was hoping you'd pick up, but…anyway, I was just thinking about the last time we saw each other. And I got so hard that I almost came just from the thought of what you did with your tongue. I'm really hoping you can do it again. Why don't you come over so you can do it again? Call me.

He hangs up and throws his phone. He begins to drink again. But this time, he may cry.
Probably. Or maybe he's too dead inside. I don't know.
Beat.
He goes to get his phone. He starts undressing and takes some provocative photos. He opens an app on his phone and posts the photos with the caption:

Hashtag nude. Hashtag my body. Hashtag COME THRU!

As soon as he posts the photos, a message immediately pops up. We see the message from:

TRADEHUNGLIKEAHORSE_99. "U look sexy as fuck"

#1. *(As Donté, smiles, genuinely, before typing:)* "Thanks. So do you."

TRADEHUNGLIKEAHORSE_99. "Dats wassup u trynna fuck"

#1. *(As Donté, smiles even harder, then replies:)* "Straight to the point I see."

TRADEHUNGLIKEAHORSE_99. "Yeah so wassup"

#1. *(As Donté.)* "Yeah, I really wanna fuck."

TRADEHUNGLIKEAHORSE_99. "Where u live"

#1. *(As Donté, replies:)* "000 0 Street Avenue Boulevard Drive"

TRADEHUNGLIKEAHORSE_99. "Im not dat far away b there n 2 minutes"
(Immediately sends another message:) "I dont fuck wit dirty dicks u clean"

> *A moment. Donté is conflicted about how to respond. He makes a decision.*

#1. *(As Donté, types.)* "Yeah, I'm clean."

TRADEHUNGLIKEAHORSE_99. "Dats wassup Im outside"

> *Donté quickly finishes the bottle. Then he puts on some cologne and pops a mint. He puts on music. Something like Jodeci's "Freek'n You," or TLC's "Red Light Special" maybe.**
> *There's a knock on the door. Donté answers. It's Trade. Maybe he wears Timbs and a fitted. He enters.*

#1. *(As Donté.)* That was fast.

#2. *(As Trade.)* I wasn't dat far away.

#1. *(As Donté.)* That's convenient. Are you thirsty or hungry?

> *Trade licks his lips and lustfully stares at Donté.*

I'm Donté.

#2. *(As Trade.)* Dat's wassup.

#1. *(As Donté.)* Um… So…what's your name?

#2. *(As Trade.)* Trade Hung Like A Horse Underscore 99.

#1. *(As Donté.)* That's a really nice name.

#2. *(As Trade.)* Thanks. It run in the family. Can I light up in here?

#1. *(As Donté.)* Um?

* See Note on Songs/Recordings at the back of this volume.

#2. *(As Trade.)* I read that some studies say weed a aphrodisiac. Say it heighten touch like a muh'fucka, that it put you aaaaaall the way in ya body. 'Specially when you 'bout ta…

He may motion "bussin' a nut."

#1. *(As Donté.)* Well. I mean. Since you put it that way.

Trade pulls out weed, a blunt, and a razor. He begins to roll an L. Awkward silence as he rolls.

So, uh, what do you do?

#2. *(As Trade.)* What you mean?

#1. *(As Donté.)* Like in life. What do you do?

#2. *(As Trade.)* A little bit of this and a little bit of that.

#1. *(As Donté.)* Oh.

More silence as Trade rolls the L.

I write. I'm a playwright.

#2. *(As Trade.)* Dat's wassup. Shakespeare dat nigga.

Trade smokes.

#1. *(As Donté.)* You write?

#2. *(As Trade.)* Like a muh'fucka.

#1. *(As Donté.)* What do you write?

#2. *(As Trade.)* The same shit all niggas write.

#1. *(As Donté.)* Oh.

#2. *(As Trade.)* The plight of the Black community. The prison-industrial complex. Police brutality. Toxic masculinity. Rape culture. Counterculture. Doin' It 4 Da Culture. Da mamas dat be birthin' the cultures. Mamas on the sofa wonderin', "Oh Lordy, why you make my life so hard?" Since four of her seven kids fell victim to the crack epidemic while under the Reagan administration. How her one child, who was destined for promise, started sellin' crack then got shot and killed. How so many niggas in jail, and got their rights revoked, for sellin' weed, but now corporations makin' a profit off dat shit. How niggas smoke weed to numb the pain. The hike of suicide in our community. Oh yeah, and Black Death 'cause dat's the shit that gets produced. I normally do it through Greek tragedy, but I'm kinda tryin' absurdism now. Dat's the kinda shit I write. What you write about?

Trade passes the L to Donté, who begins to smoke.

#1. *(As Donté.)* Um. That.

#2. *(As Trade.)* Dat's wassup.

They smoke. They're high.

So, wassup?

#1. *(As Donté.)* Wassup?

#2. *(As Trade.)* Birds.

#1. *(As Donté.)* And trees.

#2. *(As Trade.)* And firefighters climbin' up tall ass ladders to get to cryin' ass babies at the top of a burnin' buildin'.

#1. *(As Donté.)* And the sky.

#2. *(As Trade.)* Yeah…the sky.

#1. *(As Donté.)* That really is what is up.

#2. *(As Trade.)* Plus, it's blue…and this dick is hard so, nigga, what you gonna do?

Beat.
Donté gets on his knees. He starts undoing Trade's pants, and then he starts sucking his dick.
He pulls Trade's pants down more and gets on top of him, as he pulls his own pants down, too.
It looks like he's about to ride him. He reaches for a condom.

Nah. No condom. I don't like how that shit feel.

Not knowing what to do, Donté freezes, until…
Trade switches positions with him and starts riding him.
From the way they're moaning, you can tell this may be the best sex they've ever had.
They fuck for what feels like forever.
Then…
They finish.
They lay there quiet and sweaty, as The Numbers increase.
Then:

#1. *(As Donté.)* Wow.

#2. *(As Trade.)* Yeah.

#1. *(As Donté.)* That was…wow.

#2. *(As Trade.)* Yeah.

#1. *(As Donté.)* We have to do that again sometime.

#2. *(As Trade.)* Nah.

#1. *(As Donté.)* Oh.

#2. *(As Trade.)* I mean, dat fuck was amazin'. Like…damn. And you sexy and all, but ya eyes sad. And I feel like dat shit might jump on me.

#1. *(As Donté.)* Oh.

#2. *(As Trade.)* Yeah, it's no shade. But… I'm out.

Trade puts his clothes on and leaves.
Donté stands there halfway clothed and completely exposed.
He grabs a bottle and drinks.
As he does, #3 enters as the nurse. The nurse puts a needle in Donté's arm.
Maybe the space becomes a clinic, or maybe it stays exactly as it is, and everything just starts to blur together.

#3. *(As Nurse.)* Come on, Donté. Come on.

#1. *(As Donté, drunk?)* Huh?! What's, what's happening?

#3. *(As Nurse.)* Bloodwork.

#1. *(As Donté.)* Oh. Yeah. My favorite time of the year. Hooray!

#3. *(As Nurse.)* Almost done, sweetie.

#1. *(As Donté.)* No rush. This has become a highlight. Having to fill one, two, three, four, five, six, seven, eight, nine. Wow. Nine tubes. All with my blood. Drain away, Nurse.

#3. *(As Nurse.)* Are you doing okay, Donté?

#1. *(As Donté.)* Never been better. BECAUSE! A pill a day keeps the AIDS away!

#3. *(As Nurse.)* You sure you doing okay, honey? You miss appointments and you know that's a big "no-no," if you want your viral load to stay low if you want to be undetectable, and your CD4 count to stay high if you want to stay healthy. And it's just…whenever you do come, you're usually…you're usually drunk.

#1. *(As Donté.)* Not true. The last time I was here, a few months ago, I wasn't drunk. I was high. The trade I messed with put me on to Mary Jane. *(Sings like the Rick James song:) Do ya, do ya, do ya, do ya, do ya, do ya really think ya love me, Mary Jane?*

#3. *(As Nurse.)* Donté, I'm curious, just in case you ever need it, do you have anyone you can talk to?

#1. *(As Donté.)* I have *you.*

#3. *(As Nurse.)* But you just see me a few times a year for bloodwork, and that's if you even show up. Donté, sweetie, you aren't alone in this. I'm sure it may feel like you are, but you aren't. Okay? Look, one in eleven white gay or bisexual men will be diagnosed in their lifetime. For gay or bisexual Latino men, it's one in four. And it's one in two for you. So, like I said, you aren't alone. I see so many people come in here disheveled like you all the time. And I'm going to tell you something I say to them when they miss appointments, don't take their meds, and find themselves drunk more often than not, *"Sometimes the hurt is a bigger virus than the HIV."*

> *The nurse finishes Donté's bloodwork, she removes the needle from his arm.*

Hope that didn't hurt, honey. Welp, I'm all done. Now all gone.

> *And with that, the nurse is gone.*
> *Alone again, Donté just stands there. He grabs a bottle and drinks.*
> *There's a knock on the door. He goes over to answer it.*

#1. *(As Donté.)* Who is it?

#2. *(As ______.)* It's me.

#1. *(As Donté.)* Mom?

#2. *(As Mom.)* Yes.

> *Donté quickly hides the bottle, then opens the door. #2, as Mom, enters holding groceries and dozens of packs of water.*

#1. *(As Donté.)* What are you doing here?

#2. *(As Mom.)* The market had a sale on waters, so I got some for you!

#1. *(As Donté.)* Thanks.

#2. *(As Mom.)* Of course. You need to stay healthy. Healthy, healthy, healthy. Have you been taking your medicine?

#1. *(As Donté, lying?)* Yes.

#2. *(As Mom.)* Good. Good, good, good. Now you have these bottles of water to wash it all down. Did I tell you it was on sale? And the lady at the register said it's the best water out there. Jackpot!

#1. *(As Donté.)* It's water, Mom.

#2. *(As Mom.)* But the minerals and the nutrients in it. Oh my God! You're gonna be so healthy.

Donté just smiles.

(As Mom.) And now that your new doctor prescribed you meds that don't give you those horrible side effects. My God. I get so upset just thinking about when you first started to take your medicine and how that pill you would take made your ankles swell up so bad you could hardly walk. I'm still so upset by that. You missed a month of work. Ya dad and I had to dip into our savings to help you make it through. And all the while, your old doctor kept saying that it was probably something you were doing, something you were taking with the meds. Not the meds itself, but you. Asshole. Ugh. Let me not get myself worked up. All is good now. That's what matters.

Donté just smiles.

Did I tell you I started volunteering for the AIDS Walk? I make phone calls to see if people want to donate money. It's really nice. I speak to some sweet people. There's a lady there who volunteers with me. Mom Number Two. She's so…encouraging. She lost her son at the height of the epidemic. And she had to do everything on her own. Damn near carried her son out the hospital because nobody wanted to touch him, and she said hardly anyone came to the funeral because everyone was scared they could still catch it. She said no one came to visit her for two months because they thought AIDS was on her walls, her sofa, her clothes. She lost her only son and for two months after she sat in that house alone. Grieving, crying out, and no ears to hear her or shoulders to lean on. My God. But seeing her now, you would never think that was her story. You really wouldn't. All she does now is smile. It's beyond me. How does a mom go on after losing their child? How?

Beat.

You can't go anywhere, Donté. You can't. I need you. You hear me?

Donté just smiles. Beat.

(Maybe wiping her eyes.) Whew. I'm sorry. I didn't see that coming. I'm just blabbering on. How are you feeling? You know what? I was thinking. Maybe you should go back to that program, that center. You haven't been in a while. Maybe talking to them might—

#1. *(As Donté.)* You just keep going on and on and on, talking about some "miracle" water that was on sale and some guy who died of AIDS. That's not what I need right now, Mom. I just need… I just need all this to fucking stop.

A moment.

#2. *(As _____.)* Who the fuck you think you talkin' to?

#1. *(As Donté.)* …

#2. *(As _____.)* …

#1. *(As Donté.)* …

#2. *(As _____.)* …

#1. *(As Donté.)* Wait, wait, wait. Now you're Banjii Cunt at the Center? I thought you were my…

#2. *(As Banjii Cunt at the Center.)* Your what?

#1. *(As Donté.)* …

#2. *(As Banjii Cunt at the Center.)* …

#1. *(As Donté.)* Never mind.

Donté massages the temples of his head. #3 enters, as Married Man at the Center.

#3. *(As Married Man at the Center.)* Sorry I'm late everyone.

He sits down.

So sorry. I was just…

#2. *(As Banjii Cunt at the Center.)* What's wrong, Married Man at the Center?

Married Man at the Center says nothing. He just shakes his head.

Still?

#3. *(As Married Man at the Center.)* Still.

#2. *(As Banjii Cunt at the Center.)* I'm sorry, girl.

#3. *(As Married Man at the Center.)* I'm just tired. I'm tired of pretending that my husband's mom is dead. I'm tired of having that be the only way I can make sense of never meeting this woman that means so much to him. I'm tired of pretending that every time he talks to her or about her that it's actually a ghost, that he's hallucinating. I'm tired of *him* pretending that everything is okay. I didn't realize how tired I was until I was getting ready to come here, and I was going to get this hat, *(Points to hat on head.)* and I couldn't find it. I went to the usual spot I keep all my hats, and I couldn't find this hat. I ask my husband if he's seen it and he says, "Yeah, babe. I wore it earlier to go to the market, and I put it on the chair next to where you keep your hats." And there it was. Not even two feet away. But I snapped. I told him he's so inconsiderate and that he doesn't think about me at all, and that if he did, he would've put this hat that's on my fucking head where all of my fucking hats go. And I started yelling so loud and then crying even louder until I started laughing. I was laughing, one, to stop my crying and, two, so it could make it easier to tell him, "I'm so sorry, babe. I realized how ridiculous all that was. I'm just running late. That's all. My 'craziness' just now had nothing to do with you." We kiss, and he tells me it's cool. *It's cool.* When I left, as soon as I walk out the door, I start crying again. Not because of how tired I am, but because I realize he's probably tired, too. I realize he probably has to pretend sometimes, too. So, I'm sorry for being late, and I'm sorry for going on and on like that. I mean, can I be any more cliché while in this program? *(Notices Donté.)* Hey, Donté.

#1. *(As Donté.)* Hey.

#3. *(As Married Man at the Center.)* Long time, no see.

#2. *(As Banjii Cunt at the Center.)* I know, right. That's what I told him. And biiiiiiiiiiiiiitch, you missed it. I spilled tea earlier.

#3. *(As Married Man at the Center.)* What?

#2. *(As Banjii Cunt at the Center.)* So you know I started messin' with this guy after my parents kicked me out a few years back, right?

#3. *(As Married Man at the Center.)* Right.

#2. *(As Banjii Cunt at the Center.)* And I was so hype because he was older, had mad money or whateva, and got me a place to stay, right?

#3. *(As Married Man at the Center.)* Right.

#2. *(As Banjii Cunt at the Center.)* And how I neva reeeeeeally said nothin' 'bout him or shared who he was because he was trade and super secretive, right?

#3. *(As Married Man at the Center.)* Right.

#2. *(As Banjii Cunt at the Center.)* Well, bitch! His name is Trade Hung Like A Horse Underscore 80! And one night we out at this gay bar. It's real late, how the trade like it, so no eye'll be on 'em. Except…two eyes are on my trade. Eyes that look just like his. Eyes that stared into his eyes as soon as he came into this world. Eyes that run in the family, bitch.

#3. *(As Married Man at the Center.)* Are you saying that—

#2. *(As Banjii Cunt at the Center.)* They were his son's eyes? Yes. And they were as brown as the cross Jesus died on. You would have thought they saw the second comin'. Father and son both the trade. Both at the same bar, at the same time. Bitch, I thought it *was* the second comin'.

#3. *(As Married Man at the Center.)* And what happened?

#2. *(As Banjii Cunt at the Center.)* Neitha said a mumblin' word.

#3. *(As Married Man at the Center.)* They didn't do anything?

#2. *(As Banjii Cunt at the Center.)* Except drink. They insides was probably drownin' that night.

#3. *(As Married Man at the Center.)* And what happened after that?

#2. *(As Banjii Cunt at the Center.)* I got wit' his son. That big ole bottom. Chile, it was the best sex I ever had.

#3. *(As Married Man at the Center.)* Did the dad found out?

#2. *(As Banjii Cunt at the Center.)* Yeah. But only cuz the son got sloppy. But that's cuz my dick too bomb. It made him lose his mind. He started FaceTiming me when they were out togetha at Chuck E. Cheese and shit.

#3. *(As Married Man at the Center.)* Chuck E. Cheese? How old is the son?

#2. *(As Banjii Cunt at the Center.)* Late teens, early twenties.

#3. *(As Married Man at the Center.)* Oh.

#2. *(As Banjii Cunt at the Center.)* Family time is really important to them.

#3. *(As Married Man at the Center.)* Oh.

#2. *(As Banjii Cunt at the Center.)* But get this. After the dad found out, he snapped. Stopped payin' the rent for my apartment. Stopped answerin' my calls, and stopped being the father to his son.

#3. *(As Married Man at the Center.)* Damn.

#2. *(As Banjii Cunt at the Center.)* Right. Then the repressed hate-crime shit started happenin'. The callin' me all types of faggot. Told me they hope I get AIDS and die, and if AIDS didn't kill me first, they would. But the gag is…they can say whateva they want 'cause I can just say, "But I fucked both y'all. Father and son! Ahhhhhh!"

A moment.

Seriously, I'm tired of trade.

#3. *(As Married Man at the Center.)* I'm tired of pretending.

#2. *(As Banjii Cunt at the Center.)* The trade is always pretendin'.

#3. *(As Married Man at the Center.)* I wish pretending was a trade so I can get paid for being tired.

#2. *(As Banjii Cunt at the Center.)* I'm just tired.

#3. *(As Married Man at the Center.)* Real tired.

#2. *(As Banjii Cunt at the Center.)* So tired.

#3. *(As Married Man at the Center.)* So tired.

#2 and #3. *(As Banjii Cunt at the Center and Married Man at the Center.)* So, so, so, so, so, so, so very tired.

Beat.

You tired, Donté?

#1. *(As Donté.)* I think I'm gonna finish my play. I'm gonna make the man kill himself.

#2 and #3. *(As Banjii Cunt at the Center and Married Man at the Center.)* Huh?

#1. *(As Donté.)* Nothing.

A moment.

I need a drink.

The space becomes the bar we saw earlier. #1 and #3 position themselves exactly as we saw them earlier, as #2 exits the playing space.

(As Donté, to Bartender, super drunk.) Hey, hey, hey. HEY!

#3. *(As Bartender.)* Yes, Donté.

#1. *(As Donté.)* When I was little, I useta show my dick to my friends all the time. You ever do that, Bartender?

#3. *(As Bartender.)* Yeah.

#1. *(As Donté.)* You wanna, you wanna see my dick?

#3. *(As Bartender.)* As much as I would love to, I gotta get other people feeling good, too. Not just you.

#2 walks in and sits. Bartender goes over to him.

Hey, how can I help you?

#2. *(As Person at Bar.)* Just a beer.

#3. *(As Bartender.)* You got it.

Bartender goes to get a beer for Person at Bar. He gives Person at Bar the beer.

#2. *(As Person at Bar.)* Thanks.

Donté goes and sits next to Person at Bar.

#1. *(As Donté.)* Hey!

#2. *(As Person at Bar.)* Hi.

#1. *(As Donté.)* I've never seen you here before.

#2. *(As Person at Bar.)* That's 'cause…

#2 breaks the scene.

(As #2, to #1, concerned.) Are you okay? Do you need to take a break or anything? Or like, use the safe word?

#3. Come on, Number Two. What are you doing?!

#1. Nah, it's cool. I'm cool.

#2. You sure? It's been pretty intense. And it's about to intensify.

#1. I'm sure. We can keep going.

#2 gently grabs #1's hand, a moment.

#2. Okay.

#1. I'll start us over. *(As Donté.)* I've never seen you here before.

#2. *(As Person at Bar.)* That's 'cause I've never been here before.

#1. *(As Donté.)* Makes sense. I'm Donté.

#2. *(As Person at Bar.)* And I'm Person at Bar.

#1. *(As Donté.)* Well…it's nice to meet you, Person at Bar.

#2. *(As Person at Bar.)* And it's nice to meet you, Donté.

Donté smiles.

You have a pretty smile.

#1. *(As Donté.)* Thanks. I almost forgot what it looks like.

#2. *(As Person at Bar.)* Why's that?

#1. *(As Donté.)* I don't know. I feel like the only time we truly ever smiled was when we were little kids. Like, real little. That's probably when we were the most carefree and happiest, maybe.

#2. *(As Person at Bar.)* Maybe.

Donté drinks.

#1. *(As Donté.)* Can I ask you a kinda personal question?

#2. *(As Person at Bar, nervous.)* Suuuure.

#1. *(As Donté.)* What do you want out of life?

#2. *(As Person at Bar.)* Like existentially or personally?

#1. *(As Donté.)* Whatever.

#2. *(As Person at Bar.)* I don't think I know. How about you?

#1. *(As Donté.)* I want to like myself. That would be nice.

#2. *(As Person at Bar.)* Excuse me?

#1. *(As Donté.)* Nothing.

Donté drinks. He falls. Person at Bar helps him up.

#2. *(As Person at Bar.)* Are you okay?

#1. *(As Donté.)* Never been better.

He drinks.

Hey!

#2. *(As Person at Bar.)* Yes.

#1. *(As Donté.)* When I was little, I useta show my dick to my friends all the time. You ever do that, Person at Bar?

#3. *(As Bartender, trying to calm Donté.)* Aye, Donté.

#2. *(As Person at Bar.)* I think, I think you may have had too much to drink.

#1. *(As Donté.)* No, I haven't. I've got pure vodka running through my veins. I'm not a lightweight.

#2. *(As Person at Bar.)* Okay.

#1. *(As Donté.)* My dick is the same size as your beer bottle. Look. Let me show you.

Donté gets up and starts undoing his pants.
Bartender rushes over to him.

#3. *(As Bartender.)* Hey!

#1. *(As Donté.)* Hey, Bartender! Hey!

#3. *(As Bartender.)* We don't want to show the whole world *your* beer bottle. 'Cause if you do, then no one would come in here to drink. Then I'd be out of a job. We don't want that.

#1. *(As Donté.)* No, we don't.

#3. *(As Bartender.)* What we do want is for you to go home and get some rest. Okay?

#1. *(As Donté.)* Okay.

#3. *(As Bartender.)* Go straight home, and get straight in bed. Okay?

#1. *(As Donté.)* Okay. I'll see you tomorrow.

#3. *(As Bartender.)* How about next week. Okay?

#1. *(As Donté.)* Okay.

Beat.

You may not even see me then. Okay?

#3. *(As Bartender.)* Okay.

#1. *(As Donté, definitely.)* Okay.

#2 and #3 exit the playing space.
Donté, alone at home, runs a bath. As the bath runs, he makes a call and puts the phone on speaker.
It rings.

Don't pick up, don't pick up, don't pick up.

The call goes to voicemail.

VOICEMAIL. *(#2, as Mom.) Hi, this is Mom. I can't come to the phone right now. I'm probably volunteering for a noble cause that you should donate to! What you should also do is leave a brief message. I'd really appreciate it. And if this is Donté, Mommy loves you, baby. A whole lot. And don't forget to eat. BEEP!*

#1. *(As Donté.)* Hi, Mom. It's me, Donté. I was just calling to say, "Hi." So…hi.

Pause.

I'm actually about to take a bath. While I was letting the water run, this huge breeze blew through the opening in my window. It was so, like, forceful that it scared the crap outta me. After I realized it was just a gust of wind that scared me like that, I started laughing so hard. Then I thought of you. I thought about that time we were watching some movie in the living room. I really don't remember what movie it was. I just remember halfway through a gust a wind pushed through the open window, but the blinds were closed, so the wind made the blinds shudder like someone was trying to break in. You remember that? You remember you got so scared that you ran upstairs? Your reaction was so quick and impulsive that you left me there. For like three seconds I didn't know what to do. Then I ran after you. Then Dad looked to see what it was and realized it was just the wind. You remember that? All that commotion because of a breeze. We all laughed afterward, but I remember looking at you. You were laughing, but you had this look on your face like, "I can't believe I ran and left my baby. What kinda mother would do that?" But you just kept laughing. Even though I can tell you felt so bad, like the worst mom ever.

Pause.

I want you to know, you aren't a bad mom. You're actually the best mom I could have ever had. Ever.

Pause.

Well… I just wanted you to know that. I think my bath is done, so I'm about to get in. I love you, Mom. And please change your answering machine!

Donté hangs up. He grabs a bottle of pills and takes them all. He takes off his clothes then gets in the bath.

As The Numbers increase, he just floats.

Andf l o a t s.

A n d f l o a t s .

Then…

He doesn't.

He stops moving.

Beat.

He pops up.

(As Donté.) Niggaaaaaa! Niggaaaaaaa!
I don't want to do this anymore.
I can't do this anymore.

Waiting room music may play. #2 and #3 enter.

#3. But, but you have to.

#1. *(As Donté?)* No, I don't. Let's…let's change the rules. Let's start over. Please. Take me, take me back to when I was a little boy. And we were playing. And everything was a game, and nothing was real. I just really wanna go back to that time! Please.

They say nothing.

(As #1.) Please. Please. Please!

#3. I'm sorry, man, but…we, we can't.

#1. Yes, we can. Let's go back to that, to then. Please. Please.

They say nothing.

#2. I got it!

#3. What?

#2 goes up to #1.

#2. You can meet somebody instead?!

#3. He can?

#2. Yes!

#3. That's not how this goes.

#2. Well, it will today. *(To #1.)* You'll meet someone who'll feel so… familiar.

#1. I will?

#2. Yeah. And he'll make you feel like you've known him your entire life, but you'll have just met him.

#1. Really?

#2. Yeah. And his name'll be... *(Thinking.)* ...Man of Your Dreams!

#1. Really?

#2. Yeah. And... And...you two will get married!

#2 falls on bended knee in front of #1.

#3. Number Two, what are you doing?!

#2. *(As Man of Your Dreams.)* Donté, I'm Man of Your Dreams and...and I want to know...will you marry me?

#1. Can this really happen?

#3. Yeah, Number Two, can it? *(Pointing to The Numbers.)* 'Cause I don't think it can!

#2. Of course it can. We can create our destiny.

#1. Really?

#2. Really...
So...
Will you marry me?

#1. *(Processing, confused.)* So...
Wait...
I'm still Donté?
And you're Man of Your Dreams?

#2. We can be whoever we want to be.
(Trying to believe what he's saying.) Yeah, mhm, we can...
Whoever we want.
(Pointing to #3.) And I want you to be Officiant of Wedding.

#3. Are you sure we can do this?

#2. Yes! Stop asking that, and let's just do it.

#1. Okay. I'll marry you.

#2. Great. Now come on Number Three. I mean, Officiant of Wedding.

#3. *(As Officiant of Wedding? Nervous.)* Okay.

Donté and Man of Your Dreams, or #1 and #2. No, it IS Donté and... You know what? I actually don't know. It's all a blur right now.
So...
Let's just say...they stand in front of Officiant of Wedding/#3.

Soooo…dearly beloveds, we are gathered here today…

The ticking gets louder.

Are you really sure we can do this?! Like, go against what's meant to be?

The ticking gets louder.

#2. Yes. What's stopping us?

#3. Life. Circumstances. Reality. No matter how much we may want it to, this story is not going to change.

#2. Maybe, maybe we aren't trying hard enough to change it. *(Pointing to The Audience.)* Maybe if we get them to—

#3. No, we're done using them! Okay? Number One, come on. We have to finish what we started. Now.

#1. No. I really don't want to. Please.

#2. You don't have to. We don't have to anymore.

#3. We don't have a choice. This ain't no game that you can cut on and off, or stop playing because it's not going your way. This is a story. Donté's story, that we *have* to tell. You don't think I get tired of having to go through this story over and over again? I do it because us telling this story, letting them see *this* reality that maybe it won't have to be our reality anymore. That maybe those numbers can stop growing. *(Pointing to The Audience.)* We're here because of them. They came to see a story. A story that has a beginning, a middle, and an END! An end to Donté's life. They like shit like that. Black Death gets through to them.

The ticking gets louder.

#2. Who is the "*them*" that you're talking about? Huh? Because… because I don't want to tell a story for those people. And if we have to, I want for us to tell it a different way. Please. We need to.

#3 looks at The Audience, then The Numbers.

#3. We don't have a choice. Now come on, Number One! It's time to die.

Desperate to help #1, #2 grabs at The Numbers.
He musters all the energy he has and tries to destroy them.
And after a valiant attempt, he does. He successfully stops The Numbers from growing.
But then…

The Numbers reappear and the ticking gets so loud that the men become paralyzed with pain.

I'm sorry, but…this…this can't happen, y'all.

#2. Yes, it can.

#3 goes over to #1.

#3. Look. I'm not trying to be a dick, but…

The ticking gets incredibly loud.
#3, overcome with fear, stares at The Numbers then the men.
Beat.
He puts #1 in a chokehold and begins to drag him to the tub.

#2. What are you doing?!

#3. He's supposed to take a bottle of prescription pills,
get in that tub, and die.
That's *his* story.
So that's what's gonna happen!

#1. No.

#3. Yes.

#1. No!

#3. I'm sorry,
But…
Yes.

#3 continues to drag #1 to the tub, but it's a challenge. #1 puts up major resistance. #1 and #3 begin to fight. They're both evenly matched, so you don't know who will win.
Until…
#2 pulls out the razor he had when he was Trade Hung Like A Horse Underscore 99.

#2. *(To #3.)* I will cut you so deep and so wide open that we'll be floating in your blood.

Pause.

#3. No, you won't.

#2. Yes, I will.

#3. No, you won't.

#2. Don't test me.

Pause. #3 continues to drag #1 to the tub.

#1. Let me go!

#2. Let him go!

#3. I'm so, so sorry, Number One, but this is how the story goes.

#1 tries to break free.

#1. Get off me!

#2. Get off him!

#1. Get the fuck off me!

#3 continues to drag #1 to the tub.

#2. Please don't do this, Number Three. Let him go. Please. Let him go. Please! I said… Let! Him! Go!

A moment.
#2 looks at The Audience, scared, then…
He lunges towards #3, stabbing him.
The ticking stops.

#3. AHHHHH! FUUUUCK!

#1. Oh shit.

#3. You really fucking cut me.

#2. I told you to let him go.

Beat.

#3. You know what… Fuck. This.

#3 begins to leave. #2 goes over to help him.

Get the fuck away from me.
Fuck you and definitely fuck you.

#3 exits the space, a moment.

#1. Thank you.

#2. Mhm.

#1. And I'm sorry about all that.

#2. Don't be.

#1. I just… I couldn't do it this time. I couldn't…die. It's like there are so many stories of people dying from AIDS, but not living with HIV. I just… I wanted to tell that story. Ya know?

#2. Yeah.

#1. So you're okay that we didn't finish the story?

#2. Yeah.

Uncertain pause.

#1. So we're done?

#2. I guess so.

#1. *(Points to The Audience.)* Should we tell them what this is or anything about ourselves?

#2. What's there to know? This is a story. Someone's story. And we're just numbers. I was Number Two, you were Number One, and he was Number Three. That's all they need to know and probably the only way they look at us anyway. Numbers. *(Pointing to The Numbers.)* Statistics.

#1. You cool?

#2. Yeah.

#1. Okay.

A moment, then:

It's just that...
You don't seem...cool.

#2. Well I am cool.

#1. Okay, cool.

A moment.

#2. Doing this is tough.

#1. Yeah, it is. Especially when you have to be Number One.

#2. Yeah. And I couldn't sit through another story like that. Especially with...

#1. With what?

#2. Nothing.

#1. No. What? You can tell me.

#2. It's just that...it's just that...

#1. "It's just that" what?

#2 can't look at #1.

#2. It's just that... *(Points to The Audience.)* they...they could've picked any one of us to be Number One. And I... I'm actually like... I'm like... Number One. Ya know? I'm like Donté.

The ticking resumes, as The Numbers continue to increase.

#1. ...

#2. ...

#1. ...

#2. ...
Nobody knows. I never talk about it. And I don't have to since everybody gets so focused on Donté anyway. Even though what was it that the nurse said? One in every two of us Black and gay men are...

He can't say it.

so...if you were...

Still can't say it.

in the story, and there were three of us telling the story, and if Number Three wasn't, then that means either I was or I wasn't. And I am... I'm... I'm one in every two.

#1 shudders.

Please don't do that.

#1. Do what?

#2. That thing you just did with your body. People always do that whenever someone just mentions...

It's pretty safe to say, it's hard for Number Two just to say the word "HIV."

It's like they're saying, *"Aw, poor thing, I'm so sorry for you."* It's like their words are so close, but their bodies let me know they're so far away or want to be. So don't do that. Don't be far away.

#1 offers his hand to hold or shoulder to lean on.

#1. Was...um...was your experience like Number One's?

#2. No...and yes.

A moment of stillness, then filling the silence:

#1. You really stabbed Number Three. I didn't think you had it in you. You're always so quiet.

#2. Yeah. I really did, didn't I?

#1. Uh, yeah. You stabbed the shit outta that nigga.

#2. I never stabbed anybody before.

#1. Well, you did today.

#2 starts to chuckle. #1 may even join in.

#2. Wanna, wanna hear a joke?

#1. Yeah.

#2. So, a man walks into a bar. It seems like he's a little drunk and should be heading home instead of a bar, but alas, there he was. He spots another man. In a corner, nursing a drink and eyeing men. He walks up to the man and bold as day says, "Let's go back to your place." And they do. When they get to the man's home, they start wildly ripping each other's clothes off all the way to the bedroom. In no time they start fucking, I mean like savage animal fucking. The bed, poor thing, seems like it's about to give out. Creak, creak, creak, creak, creak, creak, creak. So they stop. But they still hear the creaking. Creak, creak, creak, creeeeeeeeeeeeak. Suddenly, the door bursts wide open and another man storms in screaming, "I knew it. I fucking knew it." The man who was nursing the drink at the bar says to the man that picked him up at the bar, "I forgot to tell you, I'm married." And the man who walked into the bar says, "It's okay because I forgot to tell you, I have HIV!"
Dun dun dun chaaa!

Silence. #2 can't look at #1.

I, um, I heard that when I was little, maybe about six or seven, from my uncle who had to live with us. He was my mom's younger brother. And for a long time, it was just the two of them, until my uncle met this guy. He really loved him, and they were so happy together. And really gay. Like the wearing-matching-sweaters-with-their-pet-poodle-for-their-annual-Christmas-card type of gay. I would get so excited to see that card each year. It was like seeing what your future could be. Ya know?
But we stopped getting them. And eventually, my uncle moved in with us. And he looked nothing like the man in the cards. He looked

empty and sad. Especially when I overheard him tell that *"joke."* One day he gets so sad, so I ask my mom if we could make him a cake to cheer him up. And we do. She does actually. I just sit there and eat the batter. When the cake is finished, we call him into the kitchen to surprise him with it. And when he walks in, I still can't remember if he smiles or not.

All I remember is my mom giving me the knife and letting me cut pieces of the cake for us. And I remember my uncle putting whipped cream on his piece. It looked really good. I ask if I could have a piece. So he takes his fork, gets a piece from his slice, and as he's about to give me the piece, my mom quickly says, "Let me taste it." Right before she does, she makes this face. It's fear mixed with disgust. It's so quick that you could miss it, but I don't. I didn't realize what that face meant until years later.

Eventually, he begins to blur his focus, talking directly to #1 and The Audience.

I feel like I always see that face and always wonder, "Do they know about me?" "Did they find out about me somehow?" "Is that why you're staring at me like that? Or you? Or you?"

Is it?

It just feels…it just feels like *(Pointing to The Audience.)* they have to watch me. Like they made up their mind to watch me, to make sure I don't get too close, so I don't *"give them what I got."* And all the while, they keep making that fucking face.

I hate that face so much. Like, stop. Stop making that face and stop staring at me. Stop staring at me right now. Stop. I said, stop!

A moment.

#1. It's okay. Okay? It's okay.

#2. No, it's not. This is *still* an epidemic. One in two is an epidemic. But, it's like people don't care. Is it because I look the way I do? My story isn't important because I don't look like I could've been in *The Normal Heart* or *Angels in A-fucking-merica*? Is that it? Well… I just wish everyone would stop staring at me, stop "wishing me well" and do something. Anything.

Beat.

I, um, I'm sorry, it's just that… I don't wanna see that face anymore.

I just wanna be able to tell people, like my mom, without worrying about that face.

(To The Audience.) I'm sorry that we didn't finish the story. I mean, y'all took the time to come here and everything. I'm... I'm really sorry.

#1. Don't be. They'll get over it. They got *your* story instead.

#2 takes in The Numbers and then the space.

#2. But it's stuck in here, waiting to stretch beyond *this*.

Maybe he's talking about the room or maybe his mind?

I really wanna get outta here. You think we ever will?

#1, defeated by the reality of having to do this all over again, goes to grab a number from the ticket dispenser.

#1. I don't know.

#2 takes in the space again then The Numbers, as he grabs a number from the ticket dispenser.

#2. Maybe, maybe if those numbers stop growing? You think they ever will?

#1 thinks.

#1. Honestly? I don't know.

A moment.

#2. I guess we just have to wait and see, huh?

The two just wait as they watch The Numbers increase.
Tick.

Tick.

Tick.

Done

The play may seem over, but it's not. One in two Black gay men still receives an HIV diagnosis. Since The Numbers continue to grow, we have no reason to applaud. Until this statistic ends, there is no curtain call.

one in two Black gay men will be diagnosed with HIV during their lifetime.

—Centers for Disease Control and Prevention,
2016 study

PROPERTY LIST

(Use this space to create props lists for your production)

SOUND EFFECTS

(Use this space to create sound effects lists for your production)

Dear reader,

Thank you for supporting playwrights by purchasing this acting edition! You may not know that Dramatists Play Service was founded, in 1936, by the Dramatists Guild and a number of prominent play agents to protect the rights and interests of playwrights. To this day, we are still a small company committed to our partnership with the Guild, and by proxy all playwrights, established and aspiring, working in the English language.

Because of our status as a small, independent publisher, we respectfully reiterate that this text may not be distributed or copied in any way, or uploaded to any file-sharing sites, including ones you might think are private. Photocopying or electronically distributing books means both DPS and the playwright are not paid for the work, and that ultimately hurts playwrights everywhere, as our profits are shared with the Guild.

We also hope you want to perform this play! Plays are wonderful to read, but even better when seen. If you are interested in performing or producing the play, please be aware that performance rights must be obtained through Dramatists Play Service. This is true for *any* public performance, even if no one is getting paid or admission is not being charged. Again, playwrights often make their sole living from performance royalties, so performing plays without paying the royalty is ultimately a loss for a real writer.

This acting edition is the **only approved text for performance**. There may be other editions of the play available for sale from other publishers, but DPS has worked closely with the playwright to ensure this published text reflects their desired text of all future productions. If you have purchased a revised edition (sometimes referred to as other types of editions, like "Broadway Edition," or "[Year] Edition"), that is the only edition you may use for performance, unless explicitly stated in writing by Dramatists Play Service.

Finally, this script cannot be changed without written permission from Dramatists Play Service. If a production intends to change the script in any way—including casting against the writer's intentions for characters, removing or changing "bad" words, or making other cuts however small—without permission, they are breaking the law. And, perhaps more importantly, changing an artist's work. Please don't do that!

We are thrilled that this play has made it into your hands. We hope you love it as much as we do, and thank you for helping us keep the American theater alive and vital.

Note on Songs/Recordings, Images, or Other Production Design Elements

Be advised that Dramatists Play Service, Inc., neither holds the rights to nor grants permission to use any songs, recordings, images, or other design elements mentioned in the play. It is the responsibility of the producing theater/organization to obtain permission of the copyright owner(s) for any such use. Additional royalty fees may apply for the right to use copyrighted materials.

For any songs/recordings, images, or other design elements mentioned in the play, works in the public domain may be substituted. It is the producing theater/organization's responsibility to ensure the substituted work is indeed in the public domain. Dramatists Play Service, Inc., cannot advise as to whether or not a song/arrangement/recording, image, or other design element is in the public domain.

9780822241744